Fergus McGonigal lives in the Midlands with his family, his cat Cato, and bipolar disorder. He has worked with Poetry on Loan, Worcestershire Museums, Worcestershire LitFest and Fringe, the National Trust, the Churches Conservation Trust, and NHS mental health services. He's won slams, he's appeared at festivals, he has a thing for hosting poetry nights, and he was Worcestershire Poet Laureate for 2014–15. This is his fourth collection.

Writing with My Elsewhere Head

Fergus McGonigal

Bx3

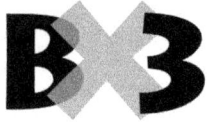

Copyright © 2019 Fergus McGonigal

The author asserts the moral right under the Copyright, Designs and Patents Act 1988 to be identified as the author of this work.

All rights reserved. No part of this publication may be reproduced, stored in a retrieval system, or transmitted, in any form or by any means without the prior written consent of the author, nor be otherwise circulated in any form of binding or cover other than that in which it is published and without a similar condition being imposed on the subsequent purchaser.

This edition published by Bx3, an imprint of Burning Eye Books 2019

www.burningeye.co.uk

@burningeyebooks

Burning Eye Books
15 West Hill, Portishead, BS20 6LG

ISBN 978-1-911570-69-1

*for Rupert Heale,
my once and always Rough Brother*

Contents

Positive Energy	9
How to Be Happy	10
Rallying Cry	11
It's My Thing	12
Whither Sleep?	13
Unexpected	14
Hymn to the Sky	16
Broken Fridge Poem	17
The Sadness of Telegraph Poles	18
Tea Situation	19
Stopping Time	20
Say It	21
Albert Camus Blues	22
Not Fully Packed	23
The Benefits of Boredom	24
Stare	25
An Explanation of British Post-War Architecture	26
Yesterday, I Held the Sky	28
and not twigs.	29
The Disappointment Shop	30
Lunacy	31
Skylark	32
Catty	33
freeform	34
Being Morrissey	35
Ultimate Bed Hair II	36
Exciting New Paint Range	38
Modull	39
I Am You Are	40
Night Walking	42

Vision	43
Sorbet	44
The Sign on the Door	45
Love Song to a Poetry Tutorial	46
No Butterflies Today	48
Disparate	49
Upturned Room	50
The Lamp Said	51
Ain't Not No Nothing (Nor Nowt)	52
Last Night's TV	53
Losing Real	54
Buy Some Milk	55
War and Peach	56
Aubade	58
Inside the Sounds	59
Age	60
Weatherbeaten	61
The Existential Bicycle Writes Again	62
Abode	64
The Universe Replied	65
Tracks	67
Breeze	68

Pieces to Be Read at a Spoken Word Event for the Surreal and Absurd

Spychiatrist's Suite	71
Cow Odyssey	77
Health Warning	81

POSITIVE ENERGY

Today, I shall be enthusiastic.
Too enthusiastic.
The louder I am,
the more insincere.

You have a new
dress/car/
shiny/tattoo/
whatever/thing?

That's fantastic.
That's just amazing.
Brilliant.
Totally awesome.

HOW TO BE HAPPY

Although he is as taciturn as ever
I tell the tree what is troubling my mind.

Ten minutes in, he still has no reply.
I carry on, not feeling in the slightest
bit mad (although I start to, just a little).

An hour in, tree clears his throat and says,
*Perhaps next time you might trouble the flowers
instead*? 'But you're a metaphor for paper,'
I say. *But flowers might cheer you up*, he answers.

'They aren't a metaphor for anything,'
I say. *They might be; you never can tell.*

I ask my cat what she thinks. *Birds. Miaow.
Beyond those thoughts, I couldn't really say.*

I start to tell the flowers what I told
the tree. We *heard*, they sang *(sang?)*. *Look at it
like this: we're pink; you're pink; we're delicate;
admit it – so are you. You're basically a flower.*

'So when I'm talking to you flowers,' I say,
'really, I'm talking to myself?' *That's right!*

And thus it was I found myself less troubled.

RALLYING CRY

Call for the generals, the guards and the gaolers,
   Call for the scrupulous crooks,
Call for the Fabergé asthma inhalers,
   Call for the unwritten books.
      Sing to the crowd,
      'I'll not be cowed!'
Make your pronouncements unreasonably loud.

Call for the cavalry riding on goats,
   Call for the times we forgot,
Call for the Admiralty's half-sunken boats,
   Call for the things that are not.
      Wave at them now,
      Give them a bow,
Turn on your heels before saying, 'Ciao!'

Call for the mysteries none can unravel,
   Riddles both unwise and vain,
Ageing quite badly, unsuited to travel
   By time, or by space, or by train.
      Look at them go
      As uphill they flow,
Thinking they're 'Yes!' when really they're '…no.'

Call for the terrible silence eternal,
   Call for the soil on your head,
Call for the loss of protection paternal,
   Call for yourself when you're dead.
      See what is done
      When you wipe out the sun:
Memories weaken, then fade one-by-one.

IT'S MY THING

after Mark Waldron

So, there I was carrying out my daily
ablutions when I reached that point involving
some cotton pads. I stood before the mirror
and, almost pleased with what I saw, began
to cleanse my handsome, nearly perfect face.
I took a cotton pad and dipped it in
some cool, clear, refreshing cleansing liquid
(bought from a store in Paris by a minion,
then flown ten thousand miles to where I was).
And as I drew the half-soaked pad across
my face, I realised that if I wanted
to buy, let's say, a thousand cotton pads
a day, then that was my prerogative.
But why stop there? I thought, I could afford
fifteen times that amount! But why stop *there*,
at fifteen thousand cotton pads a day?
I could make it my *thing* and be the man
who bought a million cotton pads a day.
I'd send my forty employees around
the world in search of cotton pads which they
could buy in crates and ship to my address.
I'd end up owning billions of the things,
my multi-hundred-million-dollar fortune
reduced to one vast, pointless cotton mountain
in which I could luxuriate forever.
I basically need saving from myself.

WHITHER SLEEP?

What time is this to be awake?
The night cut short; the stars still out;
The mind alert. For goodness' sake!
What time is this to be awake?
What chance that rest will overtake?
Is slumber out of reach? No doubt.
What time is this to be awake?
The night cut short, the stars still out.

UNEXPECTED

We hit some unexpected traffic:
a wretched five-way signal on a Sunday.
What would have been two minutes through the town
becomes a chance for conversation as
we sit, unmoving, in a queue.
A line of ornate barbed wire on a wall
diverts my driver's eye, and she exclaims,
'A modern metal crown-of-thorns-type sculpture…'
It isn't every day my wife remarks
upon the world in lines of perfectly
constructed verse. I get my notebook out.
I write the words and tell her what I'm writing:
her unintended line of chance blank verse.
'Shall I compare thee to a summer's day?
Fuck off!' she shouts. It looks far worse in print.
The Shakespeare quote was her in mock-poetic
mode; the expletive aimed at some buffoon
driving a Merc. She goes off on a rant
about the selfishness of other drivers
and then she stops. 'I've been living with you
too long,' she says. *It's good to rail against the
stupidity of others*, I reply.
It shows you're still alive. This doesn't work.
'You've imposed your stronger personality
over the course of thirty years,' she says.
'I'm now pissed off at the world – how come you
don't like ballet, or dancing…?' I'm too busy
writing this down to think of a riposte.
This doesn't go unnoticed. 'Write a poem
for me: an ode for Mother's Day; an ode
to daffodils; an ode…' and here, she tries
obscenity. *I can't write that!* I shriek
(with laughter). Now she's started, though, this
supposed student of my misanthropy
does not stop there, and launches, with both vigour
and verve, a blast of non-stop fluent swearing –
in French! – as unexpected as it is delightful.

I didn't teach you that, I think, and laugh
out loud (again). 'I like it when I make
you laugh,' she says, taking a break from swearing
in French. The traffic starts to move at last;
the moment passes, as all moments do.
We find ourselves along a different road.

HYMN TO THE SKY

That time I wrote a poem for the ~~strangeness of solitude~~ sky;
considered all its vast majestic blueness *(Note to self: am I allowed
   'blueness' here? Why is it majestic? Is it? Should I give up poetry?)*
~~imagined all the things which lay beyond~~ *(No. Try...)*
~~and contemplated worlds I'd never see~~. *(No... maybe abandon blank
   verse: too much gravitas for a Monday morning? Try free verse
   instead? What about becoming a bus driver? A self-help guru?)*
Too easily distracted by my own thoughts,
I wandered off on flights of fancy, searching
instead for words which might elucidate
this mood, this wistful melancholia. *(Why the humorous asides, then?
   Also: 'elucidate' 'melancholia'? Is that such a good idea?)*
~~There are no clouds at all, from where I sit~~
From where I sat, I saw no clouds at all,
but emptiness and ~~the next-door neighbour's bloody dog, barking,
again!!!~~ birdsong on a breeze. *(We can 'see' birdsong now, can we?
   Can we?)*
There's nothing idle about contemplation;
next time you see the sky, just see the sky.
A rush of something then changed my mood;
the night was past, my dreams all turned to ~~dust~~ sand.
Thinking about the sky, this act of looking *(This is why I prefer writing
   in the afternoon.)*
That act of getting distracted by my phone looking... thinking...
   looking... thinking...
had lifted me; ~~the day could now begin~~ the sky had lifted me.
The day began. There were no clouds, just blue.

BROKEN FRIDGE POEM

The poem hurls itself at my feet,
pleading to be written.
It is a poem about a broken fridge.

'Broken Fridge Poem,' I say,
'what makes you think
I have the time to write you?'

*You have the time to stare at clouds,
to sit and read,
to do nothing.*

'Staring at clouds is a vital part of being a poet,'
I say. 'Sitting and reading? Doing nothing?
Some things are harder than they look.'

Broken Fridge Poem looks at me.
*If you don't write me down,
it will be as if I never was.*

Broken Fridge Poem tells me his life story.
'Life stories are not poems,' I tell him,
after he's finished. 'They are novels.'

But Broken Fridge Poem
is no longer at my feet,
giving me too much detail.

He sits there on the page,
a cacophony of handwriting.

THE SADNESS OF TELEGRAPH POLES

I read a modern poem on
the sadness of telegraph poles.
It moved me greatly, and I wept
– *insert a simile here, please.*

Not enough people dwell upon
the sadness of telegraph poles,
for if they did, I feel that we
– *insert a metaphor here, now.*

If you don't like the concept of
the sadness of telegraph poles,
don't blame the poem or the poet
– *insert deficient feelings here.*

TEA SITUATION

You're so bloody weird, she said.
It had been in response
to something I had said.

She had kindly offered
to make me a cup of tea,

but the only tea
immediately visible in the kitchen
was lapsang souchong, which,
if you are unfamiliar with it,

tastes like a bonfire in a cup.

I'll go and explore the tea situation,
she said, then did an impression
of a person who very much
did not want to get up
and explore the tea situation.

'You don't have to go
and explore the tea situation,' I said.

The tea situation isn't the problem, she replied.
'It might be if it's hidden in the roof,' I said.

What's *so bloody weird* about that?

STOPPING TIME

It seems that stopping clocks cannot stop time.
I tried it just this morning. *Tick*, then *tock*
(you know what's coming next: another *tick*,
another *tock*; repeat until the end
of time). *Remove the battery*, said a thought.
Stop time. The irritating din I thus
un-dinned, allowing me some silence. *Tick*,
then *tock*. Another ticking clock to stop?
Remove the battery, said a thought. *Again?*
I thought. The irritating din I thus
un-dinned, allowing me some silence. *Tick*,
then *tock*. *How many clocks does one room need?*
I thought. Not three, but five! You might imagine
that one was quite sufficient; you'd be wrong.

How many *ticks* and *tocks* will leak from
not just one but five clocks? Four too many. Four!
I'll spare you all the details, save to say
that some time later, all the clocks were stopped.

Returning to the task in hand (a poem),
I sat in clockless silence; tickless, tockless
tranquillity. The poem wrote itself,
as poems often do, and when that final
impression on the paper had been made,
I looked towards the mess of clocks upon
the dresser. *Tick*, they didn't go, nor *tock*;
and though I had forgotten all about
the time, forgotten every second, let
each minute pass, unnoticed, into hours,
until a morning had been lost to writing,
I saw that time, too, had forgotten all
those clocks, and moved towards its destination,
regardless of the absence of clock motion.

It seems that stopping clocks cannot stop time,
though writing makes it vanish altogether.

SAY IT

Reality includes your current mood,
any bricks in your house
and whatever clothes you are now wearing,

unless you are in the shower,
in which case: reality is naked.

Reality is the pencil
which I am now holding in my hand
and without which
I would not be able to describe reality.

Reality is my wife wryly saying,
'You are quite… *focused*, shall we say,'
as this pencil does its little word dance
across the pages of my notebook.

Repeatedly saying the word reality
will lead to semantic saturation,
thus draining reality of all meaning.

Say it.

ALBERT CAMUS BLUES

Lost in the desert; no one but the sky
for company. *And when this half-light goes,*

what then? it asked. I wrote my answers in the sand
and when I was exhausted of all words

I turned and saw the wind had swept them up.
What else did you expect? I heard it mutter.

NOT FULLY PACKED

Not thirty seconds in, I said,
'Turn back.' We had forgotten something:
the summer sun had not been packed.
We found a place for him beneath
the front passenger seat. Sometimes
you have to improvise when packing,
especially when the car is full:
seven Mediterranean
thunderstorms (all safely strapped in);
a two-day heatwave (in the cool-box);
a swarm of insect bites (to give
us all something to moan about),
and the slightly guilty feeling that
one really should be doing something
other than sitting in the sun.

The sun: I can't believe we nearly
forgot to pack him. He was quite
the model passenger, not once
complaining that we'd almost left him
behind (I suppose that he was glad to
escape the gloom of Middle England),
or that he had the worst seat in
the car (*I like the shade*, he joked).
We had to let him out to stretch his
corona several times, which led
to one or two odd looks (these vanished
when sun flashed his smile. *Always works*,
he laughed). And everything was fine
for three whole weeks, despite the fact
that we forgot to pack his hat.

THE BENEFITS OF BOREDOM

The sky was English sky that day:
a patchwork stitched from drizzled grey.

With nothing else to do, we spent
all day riding different sound waves.
We started on a single note,
a C, to see if C-waves were
the same, in any way, as sea-waves.
They weren't. We braved a *leitmotif*
and used it like a rollercoaster.
We surfed on awkward intervals:
augmented fifth; diminished fourth;
precipitously balanced seventh.
Then, quite exhausted by the speed,
a silent wave of *avant-garde*
allowed us all to catch our thoughts.

STARE

I stare into faces non-stop for weeks
and ask myself if this is really wise,
like trying to catch three drunk wasps at a picnic
in jars of arsenic marked *unfit for humans*
and placed on orange plastic tablecloths
which have no place in England's countryside,
and then it's back to staring at the clouds
for what again will seem like weeks but isn't.

AN EXPLANATION OF BRITISH POST-WAR ARCHITECTURE

after Luke Kennard

young thrusting architect
v dynamic v clev
takes time from design
dog biscuit factory
to do PhD dissert
on *An Expl of Brit*
Post-W Archit
thinks:
why so shit?
what happened?
who to blame?
young thrust v clev etc archit *also*
a young thrust etc
quantum physicist
builds time machine
t mach set to 1966
town planning meeting (Birmingh)
young etc notices clothes of
chief town planner
thinks:
flared brown polyester trousers?
shirt collar size of small table?
purple paisley kipper tie?
who gave him the keys to the kingdom?
etc sets t mach to 1974
town plan meet (Middlesb)
sees chief t planner
thinks:
tie tucked into trousers?
sideburns as large as medium-sized cat?
hair by Vidal Baboon?
what sort of town did we
think he would build?
explains everything

young thrusting architect
publishes findings in much lauded PhD
recycles time machine
as kitchen appliances:
microwave oven kettle
chronologically-challenged toaster.

YESTERDAY, I HELD THE SKY

You cannot hold the sky, she said. *It isn't yours to hold, and besides, your arms aren't wide enough.* I held my arms apart and touched the horizons with my fingertips. 'But look,' I said, 'I am holding the sky.' *How heavy is it?* she asked. 'It's lighter than your first smile,' I said. Then she moved to stand beside me, stretched her arms as wide as they could go, and danced around the field on ballet tiptoes.

AND NOT TWIGS.

It took him twelve round months
to spin a nest of tables out
of hazel wood, oak, and the spaces
between the weft and weave of time
inside his wordless wooden heart.

And on the night that it was finished,
a family – of mouse and bird
and cat – lay down inside the nest
of tables, making it their home,
as unexpected as that seems.

Your protestation – 'Mouse? Bird? Cat!
What sort of family is that?' –
fell flat upon my ears. And yet
you never questioned that a nest –
a nest! – might be made from tables,

THE DISAPPOINTMENT SHOP

I walk into the disappointment shop.
Immediately, I am disappointed:
a man approaches me to ask if I
need help. 'I'm disappointed,' I explain.
'I would have thought that in a shop like yours
the service would be non-existent, so
it's rather disappointing that you offer
assistance.' Silently, he hands a card
to me. I read the words inside my head.
*The items in this shop are not for sale
at any price.* My days of petty theft
have long since passed into the realms of folklore,
so stealing's not an option as I'd surely
be caught. The shop assistant walks towards
the door and turns the key inside the lock.
I'm sorry, sir, he says. *We're shut.* I ask
if he could let me out. *You haven't bought
it yet.* I puzzle over what he's said;
I wonder what the *it* he mentions is,
then see it. Knowing that it can't be bought
(at any price), I ask if I could hold it.
The shop assistant hands it over to me
(he doesn't know how clumsy I can be).
We watch it fall upon the ground and smash.

LUNACY

The first thing that he noticed was her face,
her shy, inviting, perfect, greyish face.
He thought of how he'd like to kiss it,
but kept this foolish fancy sealed inside
his clumsy mouth. 'So far beyond my reach,'
he mumbled to himself. 'Forever and
forever and forever and forever.'

He knew that if he spoke of love to her
his tender words would fall on stony ears.
The more aloof and distant she appeared,
the more he'd fret within his sleepless heart.
He turned his back upon the moonless day,
he spurned the company of other men,
until, in time, his solitude was total.

Despairing of this life, he wrote his love
a letter, knowing that she wouldn't read it:
Your Beauty Doth Eclipse the Sun,
And Would That I Your Love Had Won,
But, Oh, Alas, Your Heart Is Made of Stone.
He looked towards the sky for one last time
and used his final breath to blow a kiss.

SKYLARK

The 'Variations on a Theme of Sound
Effects to Signify a Pratfall in
Tom and Jerry' is playing on a loop.
Or maybe it's a skylark. Looking up
to scan the sky for signs of televisions
tuned in to Cartoon Network, all I notice
are clouds. I stare at one awhile to see if
it changes shape into a television.
This fails to happen, so I search the heavens
instead for evidence of skylark. None.
I stand and scour the sky and wonder how
this bird cannot be seen when *there it is*,
as obvious as laughter in a classroom;
as obvious as skylarks in the sky.

CATTY

I read my latest poem to
the next-door neighbours' cat. He sits there,
inscrutable as weathered granite.
'Inscrutable as weathered granite?'
he says in feline disbelief.
'I simply gave your poem due
consideration while you read it.
And also, I was trying not to laugh.

'The problem with your poetry
is that it fails to answer any
questions of genuine importance:
what is the most effective way
to kill a mouse? Should rabbits be
allowed as pets? Should voluntary
euthanasia be made compulsory
for dogs? You see where you've gone wrong?'

I thank the cat for his advice,
then ask if maybe poems
can serve to broaden our horizons,
enabling us to see the world
through others' eyes: to touch their rainbows;
to hear their music, taste their tears.
'But what would be the point in that?'
he says, and wanders off in search of death.

FREEFORM

Let's break it down and hear what happens...
Rhythm, to start: a five-four beat,
played by a drummer with three left feet.

The sax joins in; hints at a tune
halfway between a wolf and the moon.
Then bass, piano, guitar: each opens

up a soundscape of seasickness.
The audience appreciate
a brave new rhythm: thirteen-eight.

Above the waves of flat-sharp notes
a piano solo barely floats,
before sinking beneath the darkness

from where a tune tries to escape,
slapped back down by a drowning bass.
It gasps for breath, then is no more

as broken fingers meet guitar:
solo from a machine workshop.
Drums now: start/stop/start/stop-stop/start/stop.

The sax brings everybody back
to somewhere near the point they started.
A full ensemble once again,

in glorious disharmony,
crash-lands from thirty thousand feet.
Silence, of sorts. Knowing applause.

BEING MORRISSEY

for Neil Laurenson

Morrissey is under an iron bridge,
tied to the back of a car.
He has a thorn in his side,
his Walkman has melted,
and his bicycle has a flat tyre.
He is feeling very sick and ill,
throwing his homework onto the fire,
and panicking.
While being criminally vulgar,
he falls out of bed, twice.
Now, he is miserable.
He jumps in front of a flying bullet,
smells the last ten seconds of life,
and knows: it's over.
Every day is like this,
in the job he never wanted.

ULTIMATE BED HAIR II

We play the latest virtual reality
sensation, *Ultimate Bed Hair II*,
and start off with the 1950s level.
You make a quite phenomenal arrangement:
*Wind Tunnel Elvis Presley Singing 'Blue
Suede Shoes'*. The world has never seen a quiff
so catastrophic, and you progress to
the 1960s level with a bonus brush.
By contrast, my *Hungover Frank Sinatra*
scores poorly, and I feel lucky to join you.
Your *Marilyn Monroe on Any Given
Morning* turns out to be a stroke of genius.
I come back strongly with *Bob Dylan
After a Coughing Fit*. The seventies
await. You choose *Progressive Rock on Acid*,
a style so vague you don't move up a level.
*John Lydon Wakes Up from a Nightmare Where
He Had to Sing 'God Save the Queen' with Paul
McCartney* gets the highest score so far,
and wins me bonus shoulder pads, with which
any monstrous eighties bed hair style
would surely give me too much of a lead
for you to catch. My *Margaret Thatcher
Mauled at the Labour Party Conference* scores
far less than I had hoped, while you, still stuck
a decade back, create *Members of the Band
Van der Graaf Generator with Their Hands
on an Actual Van de Graaff Generator*.
The score for this is stratospheric, so
we check online and learn that nobody
has ever won so many points in just
one go. *An Almost Drowned Simon Le Bon*
extends your lead. With my *Chris Morris Wig
Attacked by Mail on Sunday Journalists*,
I make some inroads, but your next creation,
George Michael Smoking Weed Crashes His Car,
incurs a massive penalty on grounds

of poor taste, and I find myself with half
a chance. *An Ageing Punk Forgets to Use
Hair Gel* sees me almost level with
your score. The final round will be decisive.
As you are in the lead, you get to choose
the order of play for this round of rounds,
decide to go first, and double-whammy me
with *Donald Trump and Boris Johnson Fight*.
I can't see any coming back from this,
and, knowing that I've surely lost, I make
a lateral move, and simply write *Post-Brexit Hair*.
We hear the strains of Morrissey's obscure
B-side, 'Hairdresser on Fire', and it's over:
I've somehow won. Conceding your
surprise defeat with grace, you load the new
latest virtual reality sensation
into the games console: *Ultimate Wardrobe
Malfunction III: Lenny Kravitz Edition.*

EXCITING NEW PAINT RANGE

Dental Hygiene
Train Timetable
Sofas
F# Minor
Injuring Crystals
Aaaaand
Necessarily
Kenneth
Shopping Spree
Repetition
Half
Instructor
Humorous Disease

MODULL

The job is difficult and skilful:
pull intellectual face (glasses).

Intense demands of being handsome:
stare into distance (point).

Some days I have to leave my stubble:
laugh at nothing (big jumpers).

It's not a job that everyone can do:
to look nonchalant in pants (not mine)

I have no words to speak but silence:
legs on a catwalk (Paris)/face in a catalogue (Argos)

I AM YOU ARE

I am immedicable anyway. You are copywritten ideas.
I am an unstable podium. You are soft-focus meadows.
I am drifting towards. You are a coathanger.
I am books. You are the Age of Aquarius.
    One of us is a pseud.

I am an open idea. You are an uninterested onlooker.
I am an unfinished statue. You are featureless terrain.
I am unskilled in life. You are as vigilant as tattoos.
I am a workshop exit. You are inert.
    One of us is incompetent.

I am frayed down the middle. You are indecipherable.
I am rowdy, or is it wordy? You are proper hardcore.
I am the ritual of diagnosis. You are a careless hoaxer.
I am a forgery. You are almost inevitable.
    One of us is insane.

I am the liturgy of the word. You are the toast.
I am ignominy. You are unasked-for redemption.
I am lost again. You are the nearness of popcorn.
I am the neglected. You are the thought.
    One of us is target practice.

I am all about the garden furniture. You are working-class escapology.
I am an antibacterial glove. You are almost wine.
I am heat. You are the lines on a map.
I am artistic. You are bludgeoning.
    One of us is a door.

I am neat alcohol. You are an emphatic voice.
I am a heedless contrarian. You are the lottery.
I am undeniably illegible. You are respite care.
I am ssshhhh. You are pffft.
    One of us is inarticulate.

I am part-time catatonic. You are pre-emptive.
I am a scrambled foothold. You are for illustrative purposes only.
I am rockburst (look it up). You are unfinished key lime pie.
I am kleptomania. You are vertigo.
   One of us is the other.

NIGHT WALKING

    Disappearing
    From a clearing,
Waiting for a certain sound.
    Darkness growing,
    Shapeless, flowing,
Over silent, silver ground.

    Whispered only
    By a lonely
Spectre walking through the trees,
    Wordless greeting
    Echoed, fleeting
As a shadow on a breeze.

    Night unravelled
    As I travelled
Back towards my morning bed.
    Did you hear me?
    Are you near me?
Asked the echo in my head.

VISION

She did a proper double-take,
a real 'glance/look away/gasp/
look back again (with mouth agape)
and stare' number, all in the space of
one thousand-millionth of a second.

Sunbathers dozed. Two lifeguards chatted.
A mother rushed to scoop her child up
before the wave crashed. Sand was kicked
by brothers. Summer yawned fully,
and everyone enjoyed their beach.

But none of them had seen her vision.
She stared in silence at the image
walking upon the breaking surface,
far out beyond the rolling platform,
then laughed, as if for the first time.

SORBET

The half-moon lit the figure of a cat,
but when I looked again the shadows moved,
revealing nothing quite so feline as
a pot plant. Once again, I found myself
duped by the night, reflecting on the need
for proper observation from 'the poet'.
What chance of that from me? That *half-moon* wasn't even
a half-moon; any fool could see that it
was one celestial scoop of lemon sorbet.

THE SIGN ON THE DOOR

I find myself opening the door
to the Disaster Shop. Inside,
there are disasters everywhere,
and dust, and concrete, and a ceiling
which collapses every now and then.

I trip over the carpet, land,
if that's the right word, on my knees,
and ask to see the manager.
His hair is on fire, his clothes ash,
his words a yoking of the mismatched.

'Wonderful bombs. Beautiful hate,'
he signs with opposable digits.
'Speaking in thumbs,' he signs. 'Like speaking
in tongues, but somewhat less salacious.
Gorgeously dead. Gifted despair.'

Laden with thoughts of mute disaster,
I leave the shop by the wrong door,
quietly. The ceiling collapses.

LOVE SONG TO A POETRY TUTORIAL

Today, the monsters have arrived *en masse*
and you are hiding in a passageway
hypnotising your redundancy pay.

*Blank verse?! A total no-no, and lines two
and three have accidentally rhymed themselves,
but it's a weak rhyme, so we will allow it.*

Their deconstructed reconstructed verse
plays tennis with the lights turned off. They can't
complain, because they didn't bring their racquets.

*I should have said: most readers will be quite
confused by all your muddled images,
and this is great (but drop the metric feet).*

Which poets borrow voices from each other? Listen:
cadences from each mouth… are just… like this?
They accidentally use iambic feet
which make the poets bounce upon their feet?
Before the bounce disappears into normal speech patterns,
and the audience is hit in the face with a plank of triteness:
bam! Which masquerades as insight.
What's wrong with these people?
Don't they want to find their own voices?
An entire generation with the same idiolect:
maydaymaydaymayday! Facepalm, banalbanalbanal.
They know how to write poetry the same way
that you or I know how to write a Béla Bartók sonata.

*Changing targets mid-shot? Rhyming 'feet' with 'feet'?
Losing the metre? Inconsistent line-count?
You're getting there, only let down by the fact that
it seems to make sense. One last, completely irrelevant
'versic paragraph' and I'd say you're done.*

The poetry collective places its shoes
upon the smouldering hatstand. Elision
on *smouldering*; 'loose iambics' end line one.

You've totally lost them now: mission accomplished.

Elision on *totally*.

NO BUTTERFLIES TODAY

No butterflies today. No flowers.
No trees. No hills. No sunsets burning.
No wondrous awe. No insights clear
demanding to be written down
right now/right here. No wry asides.
No sharpened wit. No complex, manic rhymes.
No silence giving birth to thought.
No that. No this. No deft reveal.
No metaphors. No meanings hidden.
No eyes opaque. No new day born.
No ocean waves. No invitation.
No path. No seat. No wall. No view.
No flame alight. No scattered smile.
No shifting clouds. No banished fear.
No silent dance to undone screams.
No staring at the clock. No poets' dreams.
No book. No page. No line. No pen.
No ink. No words to say. No end.

DISPARATE

Reflecting on words I never spoke –
Real or imagined, solemn or joke –
   My mind is stirred once more
By the madness that absence always brings;
It dances foul and shrilly sings,
   Like symphonies at war.

Discordantly drowning in minor keys
The size of the sky and the Seven Seas,
   And all that's in between,
While answers we seek remain unsaid,
To chance every day until it's dead,
   In ignorance obscene.

Fill every beat from one to ten,
Breathe from the heart with loaded pen:
   The loss that always calls.
Stand with your back behind the breeze,
Silent as gaps between the trees;
   Unnoticed, sadness falls.

UPTURNED ROOM

You walk into an upturned room:
an armchair on the ceiling, plants
at forty-five degrees to horizontal,
the pictures from the wall piled up
into a Jenga tower, leaning
towards the light of an open window,
in which the fireplace is stuck.

The dining table stands upright,
its surface pressed against a wall,
whose nakedness has been revealed
by stripped wallpaper, hanging from
a standard lamp (no longer standard).
The dust has coalesced to form
the words *I Am No Longer Dust*.

You set about the task of putting things
back in their place, with one exception:
the books, suspended in mid-air,
their covers open, pages half-turned,
words lined up to jump off the page.

THE LAMP SAID

a TS Eliot cento

Let us go then, you and I,
The lamp said,
To report the behaviour of the sea monster,
Miss Nancy Ellicott,
Queen of Heaven.

And I think, again, of this place,
Of cracked cornets,
Of faint stale smells of beer,
Of sunless dry geraniums
And bats with baby faces in the violet light
And even the Abstract Entities
And other heroes of that kidney.

I smile, of course,
And I say, Cousin Harriet, here is the Boston Evening Transcript
Stirring the water in his bath
With the sword in one hand and the trowel in the other.

Talking of trivial things,
The lamp said,
Jellicle cats and dogs all must
Chill
Like a dancing bear
With seaweed in its hair.

It is impossible to say just what I mean
With words and meanings. The poetry does not matter.
I sometimes wonder if that is what Krishna meant.

AIN'T NOT NO NOTHING (NOR NOWT)

There is no weather out in space,
    There are no flowers on the moon,
There is no saving without grace,
    There are no winter storms in June,
    There are no mornings after noon,
There is no warmth in Death's embrace,
    There is no song without a tune,
There is no life without a trace.
    Announce it in a southern drawl:
    There ain't no nothing here at all.

There is no heaven in the sky,
    There are no magic beanstalk beans,
There is no *not* inside of *why?*
    There are no stains in that which cleans,
    There are no straight lines in our genes,
There is no *welcome* in *goodbye*,
    There are no ills from eating greens,
There is no ending when we die.
    Please say it in the Voice of Doom:
    There is no exit from the tomb.

There is no window to the soul,
    There are no miracles, in fact,
There is no substance to a hole,
    There are no spaces when we're packed,
    There are no sins which don't detract,
There is no view inside a bowl,
    There are no codes which can't be cracked,
There is no noise like rock 'n' roll.
    Declare these words in crystal tones:
    There is no life when all is bones.

Envoi
These things should send you round the bend,
    For life's a joke and should offend,
And surely even children know
    There is no nothing in the end.

LAST NIGHT'S TV

Two lovers carve their names in living wood;
the bold calligraphy of their hearts
displays elsewhere on other special trees.

Answers fight their way into the exam paper
for fear of being stranded in a section
of the brain which is never again accessed.

A late and uninformative thank-you
letter is tortured into existence
by a terminally disorganised child.

In one dull place, the words which might have formed
a poem struggle for coherence in
a conversation about last night's TV.

LOSING REAL

*Today it is Monday
and all the grey clouds are out
dancing like bored geography teachers.*

Fatuous identity politics,
jackboot diversity tattoos
in unexpected places.

Talent show charlatans
discover poems
on alternate weekends.

Broken-tooth chic,
car-crash epiphany
in shotgun green.

Freedom-fighting blusher,
kissing smudgy lipstick.
All stand for the national handsome.

Getspend your cash
in and on until.
Just like this.

No, me neither.

BUY SOME MILK

The piece of paper found inside
his heart was folded seven times.

We wondered at its mystery;
considered it a miracle.

Entrusted with this modern relic,
we contemplated wisdom's reach.

But what we would have thought at reading
Buy some milk, I cannot say.

WAR AND PEACH

I misread *War and Peace* as *War and Peach*,
a side-effect of reaching middle age
(and being absent-minded with regard
to the whereabouts of my reading glasses).
I pick the book up, and, with outstretched arm,
begin to read. I've always been quite wary
of books known for their *length*; if measurement's
the thing, the word we're looking for is *weight*.
A weighty tome, as if the words convey
gravitas, when, in truth, they're code for 'few
people – if any – ever read this book'.
But back to *War and Peace*. *Part One* (it reads):
War. *Part Two: Peach*. Wait – *peach?* I go and find
my glasses, return to the book, and read
the title once again. Yes: *War and Peach*.
I'm curious to know how this one goes.
I dredge through lots of bloody death and torment,
exhaust my patience, and decide to skip
to *Part Two: Peach*. The brevity is startling:
'The war was over; everything was peachy.'
That's it. One sentence. Nothing more. I scan
my shelves and pick another book, at random.
Cress of the D'Urbervilles, the tragic tale
about a naïve piece of cress who ends up
inside an egg mayonnaise sandwich at
a roadside café adjacent to Stonehenge.
I close my eyes and run my hand along
the spines of unseen books. I stop and pull
one out, open my eyes, and find that I
am holding *Fromage to Catalonia*,
George Orwell's personal account of bringing
cheddar and brie to the Spanish Civil War.
Below, I find *The Complete Works of Shakespeare*.
The book falls open at a much-read play,
Much Ado About Stuffing. I daren't look.
Instead, I read some lines from *A Midsummer
Ice Cream*. And now it's everywhere I look:

Plate Expectations sits alongside *Fried
and Prejudice*, while *Nineteen Eighty Flour,
Wuthering Bites, Jane Pear*, Evelyn Waugh's *Scoop!*
(rum and raisin edition), *Tinker, Tailor,
Soldier, Pie* and *Madame Bovrilly* have
all found a place. Professor Stephen Hawking's
A Brief History of Lime proves to be quite
impossible; I hadn't known that citrus
fruits were so difficult to understand
and I abandon reading after page
seven. I look at all the books I have
and contemplate the unexpected mysteries of life.

AUBADE

It's 4am (again) and sleep is over
until I need to be awake, when tiredness
will try its best to knock me out (again).

Before the dawn, the night is at its darkest:
the place where life's demented moods are rooted.

I wait until the morning light is here,
along with all the early morning thoughts it brings.

I've waited till the sun appears
to seek the shade of daytime's harmless fears.

INSIDE THE SOUNDS

I give up wearing glasses, watch
the sunrise crash into the clouds,
and wait until the sky fades in.

I have no words as all my thoughts
vanish inside my head, displaced
by beats and notes, guitars and lights.

I catch a beam of unshed light,
strike a match, then stand well back,
watching the flames from a safe distance.

Nothing reflects off nothing, jumps
aside (waving its arms), dissolves,
reacts, and waits to find its space.

I walk sideways along a bassline,
displace my *thanks but no thanks* mood,
disarm myself and swim in sleep.

I place more questions in my case,
carry my thoughts inside a box,
laugh like a coffin, breathe in sounds.

Floating in minor chords, awoken
by pianos, folded into masks.
Something occurs (I don't know what).

I land in silence, walk around it,
inspect its lack of empty whatness.
Go back to wearing glasses. Read.

AGE

We never count the seconds, though they race
ahead and pull us in their wake. We face
the clock, reflections mirrored in its glass.
We never count the seconds as they pass.

All watches count; the minutes quickly turn
around their circles. As they do, we learn
we are impatient – minutes leave our lives
the minute that they enter. Thus arrives

the hour: a small, well-tended plot. We mark
our hours with bells and listen to their stark,
repeated question: *Do I toll for you?*
The midnight hour will bring to us a new

substantial day, and days can be like friends:
we name them, live for them, and each day lends
some meaning to our lives. We count the days,
but only when we wish we could erase

them. Weeks arise from ashes left behind
by seven days of living. They remind
us that the months are on their way, and soon
we find we have no need of clocks; the moon

can mark the passing time. Full moon appears
twelve nights and now we count aloud in years.
On years, those heavyweights of time, we thrive:
the more we have, the more we are alive.

WEATHERBEATEN

Graveyard sky
rains on threadbare landscape.

Breezes sneak between
expressionless plants.

Catch winter's dissolution.
When it's gone,

it's gone.

THE EXISTENTIAL BICYCLE WRITES AGAIN

The Existential Bicycle is writing.
*A cavalcade of words along the beach
appears in wheelie arcs and unstraight lines.
The beach contains a wealth of empty space,*
he adds, fearing that writer's block has struck.
He tries his hand at automatic writing:
*What thinking is a fascist accident,
started by fools, continued by dark devils,
and swallowed by the credulous and scared?*
It's too much like philosophy, he thinks,
and not enough like poetry. Or maybe,
he thinks again, it's simply an opinion,
expressed in clumsy haste by someone angry:
neither philosophy nor poetry.
He stops his search for the profound, and turns
to look towards a neatly drawn horizon.
He falls asleep and dreams of words and words.
The whole world is poetry when he awakes,
and words are written by stars in the sky.
*Look up towards the stars to find
a new perspective. Atoms form from their
explosions. All the things we see – ourselves,
and everything around us – are not new,
but are reshaped by chance on chance on chance.
Solid matter is space dressed up as substance.*

*

The Existential Bicycle woke up
on the Sandiest Beach in the Whole World.
The endless shore was empty; solitude
his one companion. Up he got to cycle,
but found that he was writing on the sand
in giant, swirling arcs of wheelie lines:
*This cage will set you free. Its iron bars
will give you something firm to contemplate:*

angular lines to gild Dystopia,
cylindrical, restrictive, cold and solid;
its see-though shapes will lead your mind elsewhere.
You fill the emptiness inside the cage
with unseen words; the magic ink of thoughts.
He wasn't sure what any of it meant,
but wrote it anyway. He used to dream
of cycling on the flats of Holland,
or Norfolk: anywhere which was denuded
of hills, those enemies of bikely balance,
but now he rarely thinks of them:
the level surfaces; the lack of inclines.
He writes his way to freedom, line by line,
each day's endeavours swept away
at night, by winds which bring the next day's words.

ABODE

The empty house,
where no one lived,
was built
for no reason.

Its walls absorbed no sounds.
Of children playing.
Of lullabies sung.
Of evening laughter.

Its best view
was left undiscovered,
like the words
in an unwritten poem.

Unmade memories
stood still
on floors
where silence walked.

The pallid garden's
bloodless bloom
met stillness
on each angular plane.

Time slid over
its solid geometry
until the house
no longer existed.

THE UNIVERSE REPLIED

I stared up at the January night,
sprinkled with stars whose magic, long-lost light
I still could see, and thought again how far
apart two points which seemed so close could be.

Oblivious to now, I looked around
the sky, astonished at the scale of what I found:
too far! Too wide! *The furthest point you see
is still your home*, the Universe replied.

Father and Son

A father discovered his son
staring out of the window.
What are you looking at? he asked.

'I don't know, really,'
replied the son. 'Just… things, I suppose.
Nothing in particular.'

But what can you see? asked the father.
'One thing at a time: some grass, a tree,
the swings, grey clouds, a path… things.'

The father went to the window
and looked out,
peering over his son's shoulder.

'What can *you* see?' asked the son.
The passing of time, replied the father,
as he ruffled his son's hair for the last time.

But when the boy turned to give his father a hug,
he found that he was by himself,
and was himself a man.

TRACKS

for Jon Bowen

You walk on tracks that are and tracks that aren't.
The tracks that are lead up and up, until
you see that big reveal. And it's the view,
not tired legs, which makes you pause, reflect,
converse, before you set off down the tracks
that might have been, but aren't; the tracks that do
not lead to anywhere but unexpected
places: scree slopes, grey faces, pathless halts,
sheer drops, those undrawn lines you shouldn't cross,
until you find you have to turn around.
Footsteps can't be retraced, and so you take
a track that might be, may be, should be… is,
that takes you to your breathless destination:
the ending point. That place where you began.

BREEZE

First in, then out. He found it needed
no practice; even consciousness
was not required. Arrived a day,
a day of windless heat, when breathing,
he saw, breathing was all he had.
I am but breath and nothing more.

Upon his bed he'd lain, and breathed
an exhalation so complete
it was as if the world had paused,
and at its end he felt a peace.
This is not death, or life's release;
this is myself revealed to me.

And through this strange epiphany
he learnt that things became themselves:
that some were storms, and others shade,
thunder, rain, or ray of sun.
But he would not be one of these,
for this is what he was: the breeze.

And sometimes I remember this,
when on my skin I feel a rush
of air, a breath of wind, a soft
and unassuming touch, and hope
that when at last I am myself,
I'll see that I, too, am the breeze.

PIECES TO BE READ AT A SPOKEN WORD EVENT FOR THE SURREAL AND ABSURD

SPYCHIATRIST'S SUITE

1.

I explain to my spychiatrist that I think I may have been a coffee table in a previous life/existence (one can't call being a coffee table a 'life', so I say *life* and then add *existence* as an afterthought).

'Really?' she asks.

The *no* which I offer is backed up by the explanation that I had wanted to say something suitably interesting to a person in her profession; I fear that if I tell her something as mundane as *how I feel* she might become bored. I don't want to waste her time. I tell her that the coffee-table claim had reminded me of the occasion of my First Confession (not that I am a master criminal; it's just that my parents tried to bring me up as a Catholic): the priest had asked me what sins I had committed, and I had not wanted to waste his time with a list of minor, petty infarctions.

My spychiatrist politely interrupts me with an observation. 'You mean *infractions*,' she says, and then explains the difference between the two. I am too polite to tell her that I am aware of the difference.

During my First Confession, I had been worried about disappointing the priest with a list of minor, petty infractions (infarctions is the better word), and so I told him that I like trying to bend the pins on plugs, thus making it difficult, though not impossible, to insert them into the wall sockets. The priest had asked me why I did this, which I hadn't realised was part of the bargain, so I had said the first thing which had come into my head, namely, *I don't know*.

I stop talking at this point.

The silence sits there like a poorly constructed simile.

'What happened next?' my spychiatrist asks, but I tell her that I can't remember.

I tell my spychiatrist that I secretly refer to her as my spychiatrist.

'Do you think that I am spying on you?' she asks.

I explain to her that *spychiatrist* sounds better than *psychiatrist* and am just about to add *like infarction sounds better than infractio*n, but I notice the time, gather my thoughts, and leave.

I realise, as I walk to the car, that I never shared such intimacies with my spychologist.

2.

I cannot paint and so I made a mood collage using the words which I am no longer allowed to say, but this had no effect whatsoever, so I nailed seven balloons onto the surface of a bowl of uncooked rice. No explanation is required for the failure of this approach.

I practised nodding sagely so that the next time somebody used an obscure word out of context, like *semiotics*, I would be able to disguise my discomfort by appearing like a well-practised, nodding sage. While I waited for that to happen, I disguised last night's argument as a triumph for common sense.

I pondered whether or not I would be drawn into reminiscing about the bad old days with a recently departed friend who had accidentally come to stay. This was dismissed.

Last night, I tried to discover if I was Irish. By this morning, I had misplaced this notion and so was back to being, what, English? I can't even remember my own nationality now, let alone the precise location of my father.

It is time for my spychiatrist to make some sort of sense.

'Do you think that you have you been making much sense recently?' she asks. 'For example, the last 187 words?' I explain to her that I always make sense to me, and that if other people are having difficulty making sense then they always have the option of exiting the page. Metaphorically, of course.

'But you can't exit the page...' I am not sure if this is a question, an unfinished sentence, or a taunt. I interpret it as an unfinished sentence and complete it for her. *Because*, I say. Unfortunately, I have no idea why I can't exit the page and so we are stuck, the spychiatrist and I, in the unspoken space of my own cognitive incompetence.

I ask her if it has anything to do with penguins. I am clutching at straws. Or maybe penguins.

There is another silence. It occupies the space between us, a bit like the unwanted laughter which escapes from your lips when you are told of someone's untimely death... which is a sentence so flawed that it's difficult to know where to begin.

'Why do you think of me as your spychiatrist?' she asks, but I tell her that I have no idea what she is talking about and counter her question by asking her how she knows my thoughts.

'It rather helps that you tell me what they are,' she explains.

'Why do you think your attempts at avoiding depression failed?' my spychiatrist asks, finally making some sort of sense of the first 187 words.

But I am surprised that she has to even ask, and I rise to leave, feeling slightly guilty that I had to split an infinitive, even when not to have done so would have sounded unnatural. *Even has to ask.* Maybe it wouldn't have sounded so forced after all.

I go home and burn all of my grammar books.

3.

I explain to my spychiatrist that the phrase psychiatrist's chair is a misnomer, as it is the psychiatrist who sits in the psychiatrist's chair; the psychiatrist's patient sits in the psychiatrist's patient's chair, not in the psychiatrist's chair.

'Don't you mean *spy*chiatrist?' she asks.

I suspect humour is afoot, and I laugh. I find my laughter to be unwelcome, like a mouthful of cream bun on day four of Your Latest Diet.

My spychiatrist tells me about a new offer: All You Can Say for £150 with a free diagnosis at the end. I tell her that I can do this at home by saying all I want to my bedroom wall and then diagnosing myself as having bipolar disorder, all for less than a tenner.

We move on to the subject of medication. 'Polo mints, fruit pastilles or Jacob's cream crackers,' she says, and hands me a leaflet to read. I learn that an added benefit of Jacob's cream crackers is that they deter dragon attacks. This is news to me.

'I've been reading your book,' she says.

I have to explain to her that the spychiatrist in the book is not the same as the spychiatrist I see in front of me, and that the narrator in the book isn't really *all there*. I explain that I'm getting fed up with having to construct sentence after sentence of indirect speech, which, as the astute reader will have observed, is how I report what I have said whilst I am at the spychiatrist's. The spychiatrist is the only one of us whose speech is reported directly (apart from the odd italicised phrase which indicates direct speech from me). I explain that I don't think the spychiatrist in the book is really saying enough.

I wonder whose fault this is.

'So, you'd like me to say more in this book?' she asks.

I explain that this would be very helpful, or possibly useless, depending on what she says. And all the while she's listening to me, she isn't talking, leaving all the work to me. But such is the nature of spychiatry that I fear she may not be able to make any contribution beyond the occasional open-ended question.

'Have you noticed the time?' she asks.

I glance at the clock, get up, and leave, slamming the door on my way out. I kick the bannisters on the way down the stairs, misspelling the word banisters in my fury, and, quite literally, throw my toys out of the pram, metaphorically speaking.

Later, I realise that banister can be spelt bannister or banister, and I send my spychiatrist a can of Pepsi Max by way of apology, with a note which says, 'Don't read anything into this remark about Pepsi Max, by the way; it's just a coincidence.'

Perhaps I should feature more apology notes; they seem to be more loquacious than spychiatrists.

4.

I mention insomnia to the spychiatrist. *Insomnia*, I say.

'Insomnia?' she queries, loquacious as ever.

The *yes* of my reply doesn't seem to take the conversation further, so I elaborate, explaining that I have a problem with insomnia.

'Problem?' she counters.

Once again, I feel that the spychiatrist isn't really committing to exploring the dynamic potential of conversation and I resolve to tell her so.

'No need,' she says, 'seeing as you just said that interior monologue out loud.'

There is a pause like the pause before something about to start again.

'What is your problem with insomnia?' she asks.

I tell the spychiatrist that my problem is that I sometimes enjoy insomnia and I go on to say how I expect that everybody else comes into her room endlessly despairing about how absolutely dreadful it is to suffer from anxiety, depression, suicidal ideation, or whatever, whilst not seeing these things as the blessings which they really are. *You just have to open your eyes and your heart*, I conclude.

'Ah,' says the spychiatrist, 'you've been trolling the Dalai Lama's Twitter feed again.'

I ignore her remark on the grounds that it is not spychiatristy enough and explain how, this morning, I had gone outside at 4.37am and been struck by the variety of birdsong but the apparent absence of birds.

'Perhaps it was a recording of birdsong,' she suggests.

I had not thought of this. However, I press ahead, telling her that as I scanned the trees for signs of birds, it occurred to me that, as I could see plenty of trees but no birds, maybe it was the trees who were singing and not the birds. As I listened to the singing, I tried to match the different trilling refrains to the different trees.

I look at my spychiatrist to gauge her reaction, but she is not there as it is three o'clock in the morning and I am sitting outside in my garden waiting for the trees to start singing again.

Mindful of her last suggestion, I spend the next hour and thirty-seven minutes trying to locate the speakers.

COW ODYSSEY

1. 4/7 OF A COW'S WORTH OF RAIN

I walk down the track to talk to my good friends the sky and the fields, and notice that it has just started to rain, but only slightly. How much rain is *only slightly*? I do not know. What would I say to a pushy pedant who might ask, 'How much rain is only slightly?' I don't know. It bothers me that I would not know what to say to a pushy pedant about the amount of rain; he might think I'm being stupid or evasive.

I walk past a field, still bothered. There are seven cows in the field. Remembering that cows lie down when it is raining, I am impressed to see that while four of the cows are lying down, three remain standing. Relieved that I can rely on such a scientific basis for a calculation about the amount of rain which is currently falling, I no longer feel bothered. The next time I meet a pushy pedant who wants to know exactly what I mean by only *slightly* (with regard to rain), I can confidently assert, 'What do I mean by only *slightly*? I mean that it was precisely 4/7 of a cow's worth of rain.'

2. LEVITATING DUCK

Walking past the lake, I catch sight of a duck, levitating. I have not seen a duck managing to levitate before, so this is a surprise. Of course, I *say* levitating; the duck isn't hovering above the surface of the water in a zen-like trance, as you might imagine (well, as you might imagine if someone introduces the idea of a levitating duck into your consciousness). No, it's like this: although levitating duck's feet are partially underwater, you can definitely see his legs, so he isn't swimming, and unless his feet are resting on a submerged jetty how else can one explain his semi-hidden legs except by some sort of levitation?

I apply the same rigorous logic when searching for the truth about other impossible things.

If it looks like a figment of the imagination and acts like a figment of the imagination then it's probably a levitating duck.

3. BOVINE RAIN-GAUGE MALFUNCTION

I journey outside and find it hard not to notice that the sun is shining. Sure, there are clouds in the sky and a healthy breeze is blowing, but I still wonder whether my denim jacket is necessary. It isn't. I carry on wearing it anyway.

On my way to the lake, I notice that, according to my bovine rain gauge, it should be raining. A lot. All seven cows are sitting down. It should be raining 7/7 of a cow, which, for the meteorologically inclined mathematicians amongst you, means 100% rain. 100% rain, for those of you who are not good at numbers, means *as much rain as there could possibly be*. 100% rain. That's a lot of rain. The sun is shining.

I walk over to the cows and stare at them. The more I stare at the cows' faces, the more they look like aliens. I wonder if maybe the cows are making an existential statement: 'The sun may be shining, but we, the assembled bovine rain gauge, feel rain in our hearts. Weather is just a state of mind. Have a seat.'

I check my own internal rain gauge and learn that it is not raining.

Perhaps sunshine, healthy breezes and staring at cows combine to breed levity of the soul. Or it could be the result of avoiding alcohol and having a long lie-in.

I notice that one of the cows is now standing up.

4. DEMATERIALISING COW

It is four o'clock in the morning and raining enough for me to put my coat on. This seems to have escaped the notice of the seven cows, all of whom are standing (the idiots).

I count the idiot cows: one, two, three, four, five, six…? The seventh cow, right there before my very eyes not a second ago, has dematerialised. This is astonishing. Not only have I encountered the first ever duck to attain enlightenment (how else to explain its levitational abilities?), but now I have stumbled across another miracle of nature: dematerialising cow.

It is an extraordinary discovery and could lead to all sorts of fame-related excitement.

I count the cows again: one, two, three, four, five, six...? Yes, definitely no mistake, there are only... oh, no, hang on: seven.
It seems as though dematerialising cow is now rematerialising cow. Wait until the sceptics hear about this.

5. HORSE COW MUSIC

The theme music to *Black Beauty* is running through my head. It is being chased by Black Beauty.

Black Beauty has escaped from the music in the Lloyds TSB advert, which has driven her mad. She now believes that she is a cow.

Black Beauty notices the change of the weather in my head and lies down with all of the other cows.

The rain plays a tune.

6. THE MAGNIFICENT SEVEN COWS

As you will now know, I live near a field where seven cows reside. I walked past said field last week only to notice that they had staged a daring escape. I *say* daring, but these things are relative; what may be commonplace for you or me (opening a gate) must have taken my erstwhile bovine comrades months of preparation and planning (opening a gate without any kind of thumb, even a disposable one, must have taken some forethought).

This explains one previously unsolved mystery: the unreliability of the bovine rain gauge. Clearly they were too busy discussing escape strategies to have time to consider meteorological forecasts.

Their one oversight was to leave the gate open. This surprised me, as I had thought that all rural dwellers adhered strictly to the countryside code. The cows seemed to stick to the other articles of the code (for example, they didn't leave any litter behind at all).

Thus, I stand by the open gate and ponder. Either they were so excited at the success of their plan that they forgot to close the gate (v. unlikely) or they were planning to return at the dead of night to dig up their buried treasure (a far more reasonable explanation, given the meticulousness of these particular cows).

Perhaps it is the first step of a 'Planet of the Cows' scenario?

It's 4.37am and there's still no sign of their return (I even brought my spade). What can they be up to? It's been nearly a week.

7. BURIED TREASURE

Just this morning, as I am walking past a field of no cows, I spy a man with a metal detector. This rather proves my theory that the cows had planned to return to the field in order to dig up their buried treasure.
'Are you looking for buried treasure?' I innocently ask the man.
'Ha, ha! Yes, let's hope so, eh?'
I don't wish him an insincere good luck, but rather carry on walking with what I hope is insouciance.

So – I was right all along. But what to do? Try and find it myself? Alert the authorities? (But which ones? The authorities on Ming Dynasty vases? Maybe not.) Apprehend the metal-detecting man?

I decide, after much deliberation, to do nothing, as this is what I do best (apart, possibly, from making toast). It's an easy course of action to follow.

Whilst doing nothing, I inwardly hope that the man is unsuccessful in his bid to locate the now legendary/mythical cow treasure. I'm also wary of badgers trying to steal it for their own well-established nefarious pastimes. Badgers are secretive, untrustworthy creatures, always trying to short-change any passers-by.

Where was I?

HEALTH WARNING

In a bid to reduce the harmful effects of poetry, all poetry books are to come in plain packaging and will contain one of the following health warnings:

Poetry kills.

Poetry is highly addictive. Don't start.

Poetry can lead to a slow and painful death.

Poets die younger.

Protect children: don't make them listen to your poetry.

Poems contain benzene, nitrosamines, formaldehyde and hydrogen cyanide.

Poetry may reduce the blood flow and causes impotence.

Warning: poems are addictive.

Poetry clogs the arteries and causes heart attacks and strokes.

Quitting will improve your health.

Poetry will be banned in 2027, after a referendum in which the people voted with their pencils.

ACKNOWLEDGEMENTS

Many thanks to: Dr Lisa Brownell, Wendy Stokoe, James Green, Brenda Read-Brown, Maggie Doyle, Giovanni 'Spoz' Esposito, Clive Birnie, Bridget Hart, Harriet Evans, and Gemma and the boys. The poem 'Upturned Room' was written for the 'Tale of Two Cities' project set up by my fellow former Worcestershire Poet Laureate, Nina Lewis; thanks to her for inviting me to take part.

CPSIA information can be obtained
at www.ICGtesting.com
Printed in the USA
BVHW031715140219
540303BV00001B/69/P